Cosmic Journal

PROOF ASTROLOGY WORKS

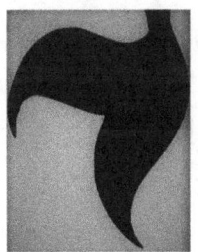

RIKKI BLYTHE

Fishtail Arts & Astrology

www.fishtailastrology.com

THANK YOU: Steve McDowell – your excellent skill of placing and positioning concepts in time and space has made this manuscript far clearer. Elsa Moon - your time and dedication to the grammatical correctness of a bunch of words also greatly, beyond measure, improved the clarity of this manuscript. Thankfully Colin Ellis - the Untangler, also came in with a fine tooth comb. Without you three, I fear, the reader may have found these ideas difficult to understand. Many thanks also go to the Ladies of the Journal Trial Group; Bridget Carter, Evelyn Jill Allison, Georgia McRae, Heather Fraser, Kerry Anderson, Joanne Armstrong, Mandy Summers, Maz Pownall, Sharon Morgan, Mary Shewa, Sue Lancaster, Valeria Siretanu; you each brought great and valuable insights to the finished product. Thank you all.

Contents

Introduction IV
Key Words VI
Where to Start! IX
You Will Need XIV
Illustration *1 XV
Illustration *2 XVI
Illustration *3 XVII
Illustration *4 XVIII
Understanding an Ephemeris XIX
Extrapolating Correct Data from a Horoscope XXII
Calculating Transits XXIII
Knowing What to Look For XXIX
Knowing What to Write XXXI
MOON TRANSITS XXXIII
SUN TRANSITS LXXXIII
MERCURY TRANSITS CI
VENUS TRANSITS CXIX
MARS TRANSITS CXXXVII
JUPITER TRANSITS CLV
SATURN TRANSITS CLXXIII
URANUS TRANSITS CXCI
NEPTUNE TRANSITS CCIX
PLUTO TRANSITS CCXXVII
NORTH NODE TRANSITS CCXLV
PREPARING FOR TRANSITS CCLXII

Introduction

For 30 years I have worked on astrology. I have met believers and I have met cynics; I said to them, "Prove it to yourself." The believers didn't need to and the cynics didn't know how. This is why I prepared Cosmic Journal; a guide for you to know when and where to look. If you wanted to see whether a bird existed, you would find out where to look. You would also find out what times that bird is likely to be in its habitat. Of course, you could hope to see this bird if it crossed your path but would you recognize it?

Objective proof provides rules so anyone can use the knowledge, to make bridges, fridges, gadgets and magnets for our wonderful modern world. Subjective proof is for one person; for example, psychology and counselling. The client is the only one who knows how the counselling helped. Psychology and counselling are similar to astrology in this respect. The astrologer – or anyone who can follow their transits - is the only one who can say, with certainty, "the Planets have an effect on me." Astrology can only be proved subjectively; you have to engage with it to know the truth. Cosmic Journal will bring to you the proof of the validity of astrology. This journaling project is for beginners, believers and cynics alike. You will discover how to follow your transits.

IF ASTROLOGY IS TRUE, IF THE PLANETS REALLY INFLUENCE US, THEN ACCEPTANCE OF THIS KNOWLEDGE WILL ALTER THE COURSE OF CIVILIZATION.

A long time ago I met a man who taught me astrology. I loved astrology. Astrology became my companion, my solace, my art and study. Then one day I thought I was mad to believe so much in astrology, so I spent two years trying to disprove it. During this time I kept strict journals of every Planet which transited my natal chart. I noted the conjunctions, squares, trines, oppositions and sextiles on every angle and every Planet in my horoscope. I watched other people's horoscopes too. Through my heartfelt attempt to disprove astrology I proved to myself that astrology works. The Planets have an influence on us that is expressed through our thoughts, ideas, inspirations, and moods.

Cosmic Journal is a journal with explicit instructions on how to track the Sun, the Moon and astrological bodies as they transit your natal Sun, Moon, Planets, Nodes and Angles. Careful observation of the transits will reveal the influences which the astrological bodies have in your life. If you do not see any connection after completing this journal you will still have been part of the research into the validity of astrology. You can contact Fishtail Arts & Astrology through the official website or Facebook page. There is a webpage dedicated to your findings and the findings of others.

Although I have found astrology to carry great validity, it is important to me that the truth is known worldwide. This is because the truth is so inspiring, so life transforming, it will alter masses of ideas between us and in ourselves. When we know that our behaviour and sense of self is influenced, despite incredible distances, our minds will broaden beyond imagination. The great truth of life will be laid bare in our times. We grow from inside till the day we die. The reality of our unity and our journey will be apparent. No longer will civilization be able to bury its head in the corrupted world of 'Me'.

Key Words

ANGLES **The east horizon, west horizon and the highest and lowest point of the Sun's journey that day. These 4 points are extremely sensitive and can only be calculated from knowing the exact time of birth. They are shown as 4 points on the horoscope: Ascendant, Descendant, M.C and I.C respectively.**

ASPECTS **The relationship between Planets and Angles as a mathematical angle for example: 90° or 120°**

ASTROLOGICAL BODIES **Sun, Moon, Mercury, Venus, Mars, Jupiter, Saturn, Uranus, Neptune, Pluto, North Node, South Node, Ascendant, Descendant, M.C and I.C. All the Planets and points in space are put into the horoscope as significant because of their position in the Ecliptic Belt. The Sun, Moon and Planets were all grouped together as 'Planets' in ancient astrology.**

CONJUNCT or CONJUNCTION **0° aspect between Planets in a natal chart as well as transiting Planets being in the exact place as a natal Planet.**

CONSTELLATION **A constellation refers to a group of stars. In this book the constellations all refer to the zodiac constellations: Aries, Taurus, Gemini and so on.**

ECLIPTIC BELT **The Sun, all the Planets and Moon are all on the same plane in space. They appear to follow the same path around the earth. The path of the Sun, from rising, culmination to rising again is a ring around the earth. This ring, the Ecliptic Belt, is where the constellations of the zodiac are. The Sun, Moon and all the Planets cycle around in this ring.**

EPHEMERIS (Astrological) **Books of tables showing the Planets' and Nodes' daily positions within the Tropical Zodiac. This is a tiny pamphlet for a year, or it is a big book when it covers 50 years but it can also be found on-**

line. An astronomical ephemeris has different data to the astrological ephemeris.

GMT **Greenwich Mean Time. All times will need converting to GMT to subsequently be converted to Sidereal Time; the time used in ephemerides (this is the plural of ephemeris).**

HOROSCOPE **Traditionally a horoscope is made up of 3 concentric circles in which the constellations and astrological bodies are placed. There are also square designs which are used in Jyotish astrology.**

HOUSE **A horoscope is divided into 12 segments in various ways. Placidus, Koch and Equal House are the main House systems. The Houses are called, 'first', 'second', 'third' and so on. Each House has a particular field of expression. The expression of 'nth' House is the same across each House system.**

NODES **In this book the Nodes always refer to the Moon's Nodes. These are points along the Ecliptic Belt at which the Sun and Moon's orbits intersect. They seemingly go backwards through the horoscope. These ancient points refer to karma (South Node) and future (North Node). They are significant to understanding some of your more deep seated tendencies which are difficult to get a handle on.**

RETROGRADE **As stated above, the Nodes go backwards; that is Retrograde. Planets also tend to appear to go backwards from our perspective on earth or they appear to stay still (though mostly they go forward – Direct). The larger Planets, due to their distance, appear Retrograde more often. This is significant when a transiting Planet is Retrograde on one of your natal Planets. In the ephemeris this is shown by R in the column of degrees of the relevant Planet. When the Planet turns direct, there is a D.**

SIDEREAL TIME **The time used by astronomers to find the position of the Planets and stars in space. An ephemeris uses sidereal time from which the Angles of the Earth in relation to the stars can be calculated. Time of birth is converted to GMT and then is converted to sidereal time.**

TRANSIT **When a Planet or Node moves to the same position on your chart as one of your natal astrological bodies.**

UT **Universal Time is the same as GMT but all year round; it never changes to BST (British Summer Time).**

Where to Start!

Start by reading through all the instructions and familiarize yourself with this new subject. The instructions are concise and won't take long to read through. Even though the principles of astrology are quite simple, the simple building blocks are used to create a different order. You are about to discover something very new.

For this journal you can use either the Tropical Zodiac horoscope or the Sidereal Zodiac horoscope. The calculations of transits are the same for either zodiac. If you are using a Sidereal horoscope you will need to subtract 24° (Ayanamsa) from each Planet's position in the tropical based ephemeris. It is easy to tell if the ephemeris is based on the Tropical Zodiac by looking at the 21st or 22nd of a month. This is when the Sun would change signs. You are probably familiar with the Sun in Aries, 21st March till 20th April. Then Taurus follows in the following month, and so forth. This is the Tropical Zodiac. The Tropical Zodiac is prevalent in the West, as are ephemerides based on the Tropical Zodiac, so chances are you have a Tropical based horoscope and ephemeris. Please do not fixate on which zodiac to use - they both work - after this study you will understand why.

It is a good idea to have your horoscope in front of you, so you can follow along as you read.

A horoscope is a snap-shot in time of the ecliptic belt with the constellations, Planets, Nodes and Angles.[1]

A horoscope is made up of 3 concentric rings. The outer ring shows the constellations. The middle ring shows the Planets, Nodes and House cusps, and subsequently shows which constellation they were in. Finally, the inner ring

---

[1] There are also asteroids, comets and Arabian Parts which can be added to the horoscope. You don't need all of these to prove astrology works, or even to reap an abundance of inner knowledge.

shows the Aspects that were formed between all the astrological bodies in that moment.

Your horoscope is like a snap-shot of the position of the Planets and constellations the moment you were born. It is like a London tube map in motion; the astrological bodies going around the centre (the birth of you on Earth) did not stop moving the moment you were born. Each Planet or Node has a cycle of its own.

The Moon travels around your horoscope once a month. The Sun, Mercury and Venus will travel a full cycle about once a year. Mars takes 2 years, Jupiter takes 12, Saturn takes 29, Uranus takes 84. Neptune and Pluto take much longer than our normal life time. The Nodes take 18 years.

When the transiting Sun conjuncts your Natal Sun, this is your birthday. Happy Birthday! Many happy returns is the ancient greeting which specifically means, many happy Solar returns – may the Sun return to the place in the sky that you were born, year after year.

Transits are when the Sun, Moon, Planets or Nodes travel to the same place in the sky as one of your natal Planets (in your horoscope). To track the transits, it is a good idea to start by working out the conjunctions. You can soon work out the other aspects.

A conjunction is an aspect. Aspects are the angles made between the astrological bodies in a natal horoscope, between horoscopes or between the heavens and your natal horoscope.

For example, aspects for the transiting Sun to your natal Sun would be: 6 months after your birthday, the transiting Sun is opposite your Natal Sun and is called an OPPOSITION (180°). 3 months before and 3 months after your birthday, the transiting Sun SQUARES (90°) your Natal Sun. 4 months before and 4 months after your birthday, the transiting Sun TRINES (120°) your Natal Sun. Only on the day when the transiting Sun is at the same place as your Natal Sun, your birthday, is it CONJUNCT (0°). [2]

For this journal, it is a good idea to begin with conjunctions so that you can begin today. A full explanation of how to calculate transits is given in the next chapter. It will not take long to pick up how to calculate the other aspects.

First, you will have noticed the pages have Roman numerals and not ordinary Arabic numerals. This is because you will not be using this book in a linear fashion. You will probably flick back and forth over the course of the next few years. Roman numerals are not so obviously linear to our modern minds; they are there to enable you to find a page easily.

The pages for Moon transits are at the beginning of the journal because you will turn to them more often. The Moon goes around the horoscope once a month. There are 3 pages for each Moon transit so you can date and review quite a few of the same transits. The other transits have only a page each. During the course of the next few years, you might not even use a page for an outer Planet's transits if you only consider conjunctions. You may choose to use other aspects for the outer Planets if no conjunctions occur over the next few years. Yet, the faster moving Planets will definitely make conjunctions. Sometimes a conjunction can happen over a few days or it comes back on itself in Retrograde and then turns Direct again, so leave space to journal that. Later on you might want to add oppositions, squares and trines to your project. When a transit occurs you need to record the results. By recording the results you will learn the influence of the Planets in your life and the profound significance of your birth horoscope. You might only need to write a few lines for a transit. Soon you will learn what you will look for when a transit happens.

---

[2] The actual conjunction of Transiting Sun on Natal Sun can be as much as 8 hours' different from a birth time. Each year is slightly different, as the Sidereal day is not 24 hours, but 23 hours and 56 minutes.

Within a year you may notice the difference when Moon conjuncts a Planet and the other Planets form harmonious or inharmonious aspects with your Natal Moon. All of this can only be known by experience and over time you will get to know the 'feel' of the different astrological bodies within you. Do not be disappointed if after a few months you do not have amazing realizations, undoubtedly it will happen soon enough. It takes time and dedication to see the influences. Within a few months you will have had some realizations regarding the Moon, which will keep your inner-eye cocked for further incidents.

This practice will also help you discern the "feel" when someone has an astrological connection with you; a study called 'synastry'. You can learn to notice what buttons someone is pressing in you. It will deepen your wonder with astrology.

Notice that the medallions for the outer Planets: Neptune and Pluto, do not contain the symbol 'conjunct'. Uranus is also one of the outer Planets. The Uranus medallions contain the 'conjunct' symbol because it will conjunct all of the astrological bodies in your natal horoscope if you have a long life.

Depending on where Neptune and Pluto are in your horoscope, they may never conjunct any other astrological body, each other or themselves. They will, throughout an average lifetime, form some aspects but that is dependent on where they are in your horoscope. Many people who are interested in mystical and new-age traditions tend to have strong outer Planet transits; they are naturally drawn to understanding a sense of transformation which comes over them. If you do not have them, it may be because your sense of transformation is naturally more fluid. Outer Planet transits conjuncting personal Planets are rare and very powerful.

It is definitely still possible to prove the validity of astrology to yourself, just by watching the personal Planets. The personal Planets are: Sun, Moon, Mercury, Venus, Mars, Jupiter and Saturn. The personal Planets affect parts of your psyche which everyone uses day to day. To understand the outer Planets you will need to look outside the box and consider a wider scope of awareness.

You Will Need

Firstly you need a list of symbols. Lists of symbols are on the following pages. (Illustration *1,*2 and *3) These make up the language of astrology. The symbols of all the Planets and transits are also on each page of the journal. The more you familiarize yourself with them the easier it will be. It will help if you copy out the symbols in order to tell the small variations apart.

You will also need a list of the Sun, Moon, Planets, Nodes and Angles *from* **your birth horoscope. There are many good places where you can get a horoscope. You can get a finely painted, hand-drawn horoscope from www.fishtailastrology.com but all you need for this journal is a birth horoscope. The example horoscope, which belongs to Henry VIII, (Illustration *4) has the list of Sun, Moon, Planets, Nodes and Angels next to it so you can see exactly which information to take from a horoscope.**

The next thing you need is an astrological ephemeris for the current year. You can buy a pamphlet for 1 year, a book for 50 years or you can find astrological ephemerides on-line. The following chapter explains how to understand an ephemeris.

Illustration *1

CONSTELLATIONS

ARIES

LEO

SAGITTARIUS

TAURUS

VIRGO

CAPRICORN

GEMINI

LIBRA

AQUARIUS

CANCER

SCORPIO

PISCES

Illustration *2

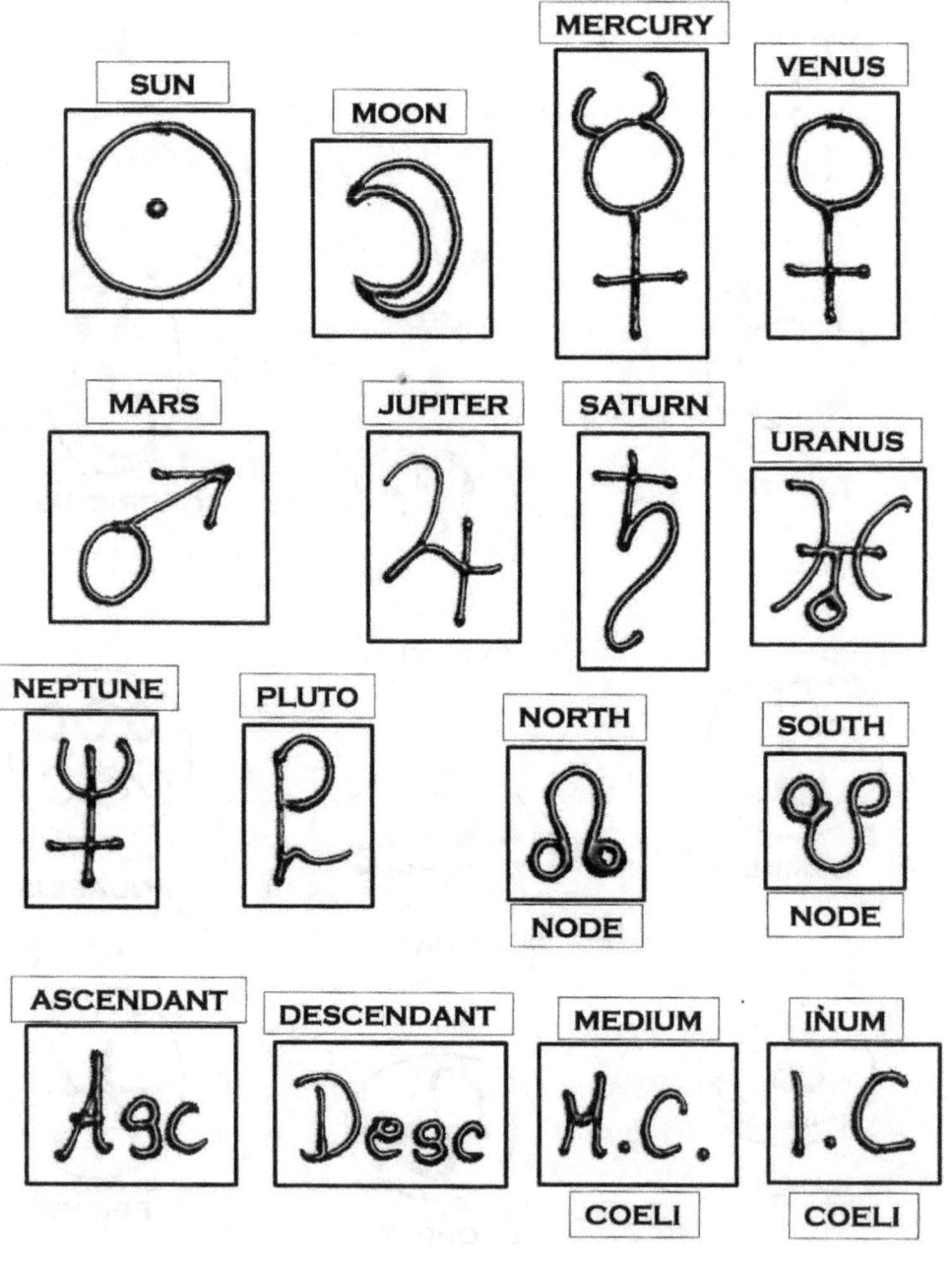

Illustration *3
SYMBOLS OF THE ASPECTS

ASPECTS

1 CONJUNCTION
2 TRINE
3 SQUARE
4 OPPOSITION
5 SEXTILE
6 BI-QUINTILE
7 QUINTILE
8 INCONJUNCT

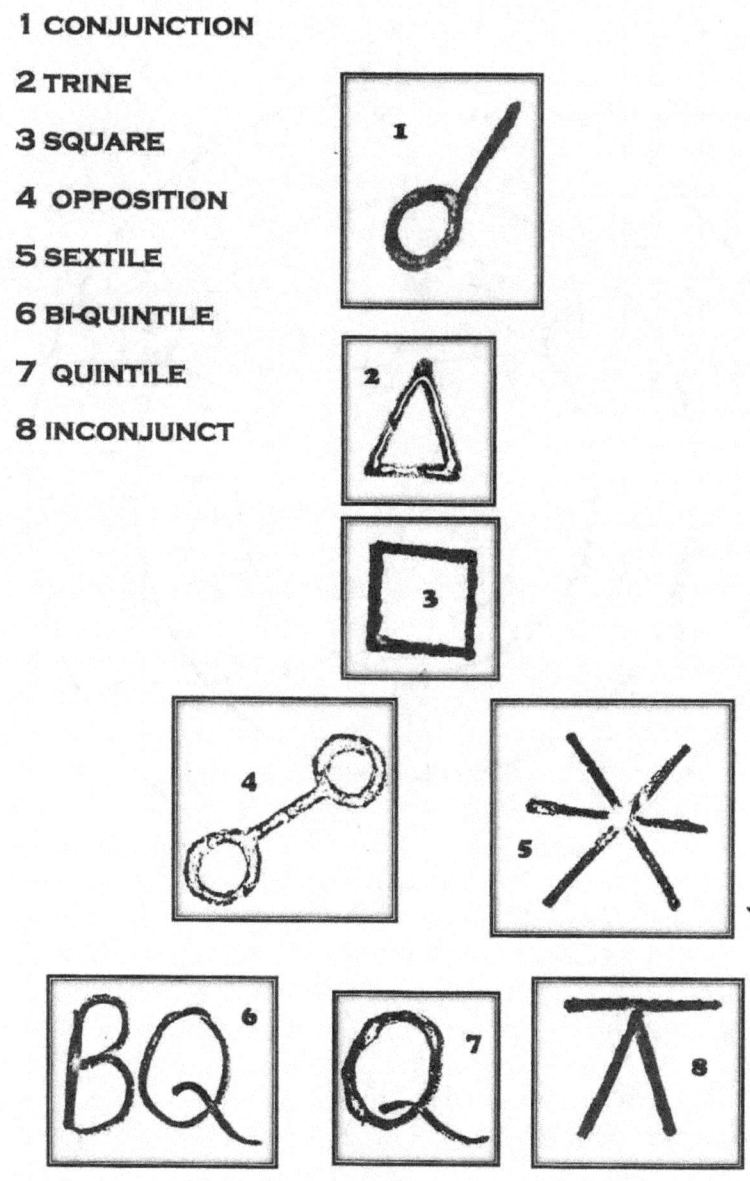

Illustration *4

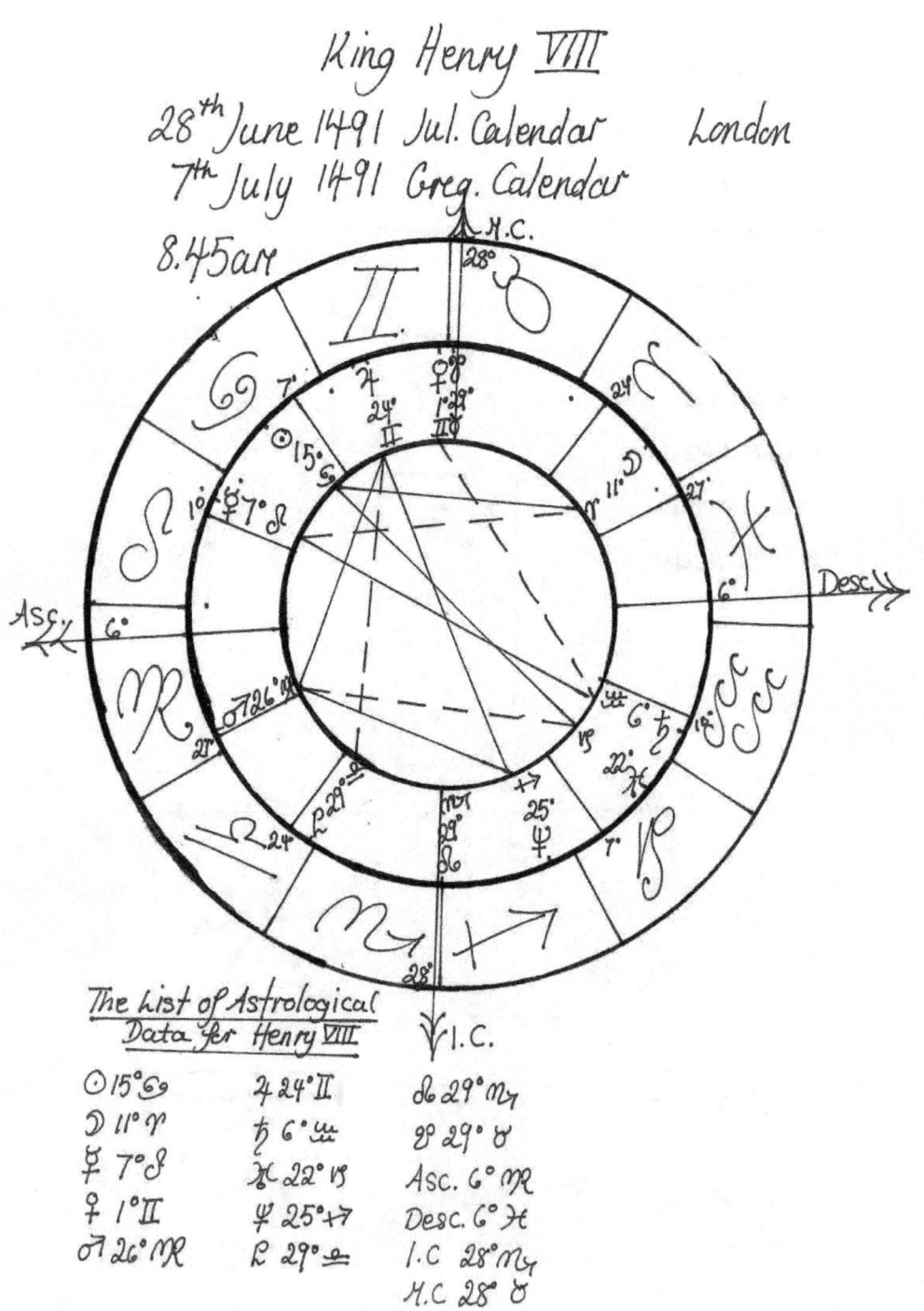

XVIII

Understanding an Ephemeris

An ephemeris contains daily tables of the positions of the astrological bodies in the astrological constellations.

The symbols of the Planets are written on the top horizontal line of the ephemeris. Compare them with the symbols on page XVI – illustration #2

The Planets, Sun, Moon and Nodes each move in different cycles. The tiny numbers in the ephemeris relate to the degree of the constellations they are in; each constellation has 30° (30° x 12 constellations = 360°) The M.C, I.C, Ascendant and Descendant are not in the ephemeris. This is because these are Angles. Angles are calculated to show the highest, lowest, east and west points of the ecliptic belt around the earth. The symbols of the constellations are on page XV – illustration #1

Some ephemerides have the motions of asteroids, midnight and noon Moon, Galactic Centre, phases of the Moon and latitudes but you do not need all of these to get started.

In the ephemeris the second column next to the date shows 3 sets of 2 numbers. This is the sidereal time for that day. Sidereal time is written in hours, minutes and seconds, as are the positions of astrological bodies in their constellations. Degrees, minutes and seconds are measured in multiples of 60. Sidereal time is also measured in multiples of 60 minutes and 24 hours, like ordinary clock time. The sidereal time is used for the calculation of a horoscope.[3] This Journal requires for a horoscope to be already drawn up so you do not need to worry about using sidereal time.

The third column shows the degree of the Sun in the constellation. The constellation is shown at the top of this column between the degrees and minutes. If the Sun

---

[3] You can access courses to learn how to manually calculate the horoscope, transits, synastry and progressions as well as to draw a horoscope from www.fishtailastrology.com/school-of-mystical-arts.

is at 20° Sagittarius and natal Venus is at 22° Sagittarius, then the astrologer will wait two days to write in the journal under 'Sun Transit conjunct Venus Natal' (the Sun averages 1° a day). Although some Planets can be effective within orbs of a few degrees, for the first astrological journal it is best to keep to the exact degree in order that the correct subjective experience can be recognized.

In some ephemerides there is another column showing the declination of Sun which is useful for knowing how close in the sky Planets pass to the Sun.

The column after the Sun shows the Moon at noon, with the constellation it is in printed between the degrees and minutes. Notice how the Moon only spends about 2¼ days in each constellation.

Sometimes, between the Moon at noon and the Moon at midnight, there are other columns showing declination of the Moon, latitude and Node. To learn how to use astrology it is best to stay simple, for now. The Moon's position at midnight, depending on whether it comes before or after the Moon at noon, is the beginning of the new day. Most ephemerides have two columns for the Moon; one at noon and one at midnight. On average the Moon moves 13° in 24 hours.

After the Moon comes the column for the transiting North Node. Sometimes it is called the Mean position, sometimes the True position. The Nodes travel Retrograde most of the time. Next along is Mercury, which incidentally is often in Retrograde and considered the cause of awry communications. Then Venus, then Mars and usually Jupiter comes after Mars. However, some ephemerides put asteroids in here. After Jupiter there are Saturn, Uranus, Neptune and Pluto.

It is important to check the time zones for the ephemerides in order to calculate the Moon's correct position. Different ephemerides use different time zones and will affect the position given for the Moon. For example: an ephemeris which uses EST, will state 'Noon' but that 'Noon' will be at 5pm GMT. The Moon would have moved approximately 2½° in that time, which is significant. If using an ephemeris for a different time zone is unavoidable, then all that needs to be done is to convert to that time zone to find the Moon's position. I do not know of any ephemeris that would show sidereal time in any other time than GMT.

You will learn how to calculate the transits in the following pages. Astrologers look in the ephemeris for future dates too and after filling in this journal you will soon discover what predictions are possible.

Extrapolating Correct Data from a Horoscope

Lay the ephemeris aside and look at your horoscope.

When you look at Illustration *4, on page XVII, you will see a list of astrological data underneath the horoscope. You will need to look at the symbol of the Astrological Body (in the middle ring) and at the symbols of the constellation (in the outer ring). Compare the symbols in Illustrations *1 & *2 to know the names of the symbols. The numbers, between the symbols, are the degrees that the astrological body is at in the given constellation.

Now if you look at the List of Astrological Data under Henry VIII's horoscope, then find the individual symbols within the middle circle, you will see that the symbols and degrees are the same.

With your own horoscope: look to the middle ring, carefully copy the symbols with their degrees. From the outer ring note the correct constellation for each symbol and make your own list.

The degree which the astrological body is at, in a given constellation, is what you will look for in the ephemeris. The ephemeris shows the degree astrological bodies are in a constellation at a given date.

Calculating Transits

You now have the list of astrological bodies from your birth horoscope and the ephemeris of the current year in front of you.

First Try Calculating Sun Transits

A transit of the Sun is when the Sun of the current year crosses the astrological bodies of your natal horoscope.

The easiest way is to start with the ephemeris of the current year, and look for your date of birth. In the 3rd column (the 1st is the date of the month, the 2nd is the sidereal time) look at the position of the Sun on your birthday. The position of the Sun is given in degrees, minutes and seconds. The constellation that the Sun is in is written between the degrees and minutes on the 1st of the month and the 21st of the month, when the Sun moves into the next sign.

Now check that the Sun in the ephemeris is at the same degree and constellation as your natal Sun. Your astrological birthday could be the day before or after your known birthday because of the difference between sidereal time and solar time. The day that the Sun is at the same degree of your natal Sun in your horoscope is the transit – Transiting Sun conjunct Natal Sun.[4]

If any other Planets, Angles or Nodes are conjunct your natal Sun, they will also be transited by the Sun on your birthday.

After recognizing the solar transit on your birthday, check to see if you have any other Planets, Nodes or Angles near the same degree as your natal Sun. They may be at a degree before or after your Natal Sun, which means transits may be a few days apart.

---

[4] There is a wonderful practice of calculating a horoscope for the coming year from the exact time the transiting Sun conjuncts the Natal Sun, in degrees, minutes and seconds. The birthday horoscope for the current year gives insight as to issues that would need to be addressed that year.

Now look to the rest of your Planets, Nodes and Angles in your natal horoscope. Using the ephemeris, match the days when the Sun will be in the same constellation and the same degree as each astrological body. These are the transits of the Sun within the year of the ephemeris.

The last few pages of this journal are for you to write the dates of the coming transits.

Calculate Moon Transits

Each month the Moon will transit all of your natal Planets, Nodes and Angles, one by one. For instance, if you have Mars in Aries, Venus in Virgo, Sun, Mercury, Jupiter, Saturn and Neptune in Libra, you will be avidly filling in the Moon transits during the two days the Moon is in Libra. The order that the Moon transits the astrological bodies is dependent on your chart.

Occasionally, the Moon conjuncts the same place twice in one month, the difference arising because the Moon's position is at the very start or very end of a given constellation. When this happens you can just write your insights onto that same page.

Look then to the column for the Moon, in the ephemeris for the current year. Is it a midnight or noon ephemeris? The ephemeris should have it written in the column of the Moon. If it does not, you will need to find it in the introduction pages or on the webpage. On average, the Moon moves 13° in 24 hours. For example: Moon moves 11°54'40" in one day and in another day it may move 13°11'09" Should you feel you need greater exactitude, just calculate the Moon's movement over the 24 or 12 hours (dependant on whether the ephemeris has midnight and noon positions), for the particular day you have in mind.

The Moon's average movement:

24 hours   13°

12 hours   6½°

6 hours   3¼°

3 hours   1½°

2 hours   1°

1 hour   ½°

Example #1: **If the Moon shown at Midnight is 13° 25' 31" Gemini and your natal North Node is 22° 50' Gemini, you would calculate the Moon's transit to 22° 50' Gemini thus:**

                                        13° 25' 31"

In 12 hours (Noon) the Moon will move   +6° 30'

Adding these gives   19° 55' 31"

To find out how much extra time you need, for the transiting Moon to conjunct the North Node after 12 hours: Natal North Node 22° 50' minus 19° 55' 31"

Note: In order to 'borrow' from the previous number you have to think ahead when subtracting degrees, minutes and seconds as they are based on 60 and not 10. (60 seconds makes 1 minute, 60 minutes makes 1 hour and so on. By adding 1 second to 23 hours, 59 minutes and 59 seconds, you get 24 hours but 24 hours is represented as 0 hours, 0 minutes and 0 seconds so you count back up again.) So right from the start, add 60 seconds and minus 1 minute from the top row.

        22° 49' 60"

       -19° 55' 31"

       29" Note: You can only go so far till you have to 'borrow' again and add 60 minutes from degree column. Thus:

       21° 109' 60"

- 19° 55' 31"

       2° 54' 29" This number is the remainder needed for the Moon to travel after 12 hours that day to the degree of Natal North Node. 2° 54' 29" is virtually 3°. The Moon takes 6 hours to move 3°. So the original 12 hours (as we started at midnight) plus the 'nearly' 6 hours means the Transiting Moon conjunct Natal North Node would be a little before 6pm that day. You then would keep an eye out from 5pm till 7pm that day for the effects of this transit. When you keep an eye out for an hour either side of the allotted time you might see cause and effect. The Planets inspire causes but it is not unusual to miss the cause and see only the effect. Astrology books give interpretations of both cause and effect.

Example #2: **The Moon at noon is 4° 55' 35" Capricorn and Natal Mars is at 1° 05' Capricorn.**

4° 55' 35"

-1° 50'

3° 05' 35" is the distance in time, on the given day, the Moon travels before noon from Natal Mars at 1° 50' Capricorn. Which means it is approximately 6am when the Transiting Moon conjuncts Natal Mars.

Example #3: **The Moon at noon is 10° 22' 31" Taurus and Natal Saturn is 16° 47' Taurus.**

This is easier because in 12 hours the Moon moves 6½° so on this day the Moon will get to about 16° 47' not much before midnight. You will be watching from about 11pm.

Example #4: **It is even easier when the Moon is 1° 20' 35" Cancer at noon and your Ascendant is 3° 15' Cancer. You need 2°; that takes about 4 hours. So you expect the transit at 4pm. You need to watch between 3pm and 5pm that day.**

You also need to remember to convert your answer which will be in Universal Time back to your Local Time.

The Moon does not transit in isolation. Although there may not be any specific link all of the time, you will probably notice that when the same Moon transits to a natal Planet in a different month, it feels slightly different. This can be because the rest of your natal chart is more in tune with the other transits and you just feel safer. For this journal, what matters is that you take note of the manifestations that occur at the time of your transits. Cosmic Journal is set out to record and order this meticulous work.

This concludes how to calculate Moon transits. You can prepare some for the month in advance and write them in the back of this journal.

Calculating Transiting Nodes and Planets

The Nodes and Planets do not move as fast as the Moon so, like the Sun, they will be on the degree of one of your Natal astrological bodies for a day or two. Like the Sun, you will watch for the effect of that transit during the whole day(s).

The larger Planets can stay longer on the same degree. For instance, Jupiter usually stays at the same degree for 5 days. It is a good idea to ear-mark the day before and the day after for monitoring the effect of transiting Jupiter on one of your Natal Planets, Angles or Nodes. Over time, you will start noticing the effects of the larger Planets, when they are within a few degrees of

your natal Planet, Node or Angle. You will notice with the larger Planets, that a new attitude is usurping your mind. You might think circumstances make it justified so you do not notice that the Cosmos and your Mind are in cahoots.

Mars can sometimes stay 2 days on a given degree. Saturn can stay a month or a week. Saturn might go back and forth over a certain degree over months. Uranus, Neptune and Pluto are similar and also take longer going back and forth. These remote Planets cause significant changes within your psyche that you will be pleased, as you go through one of their transformations, to see that there is some reason behind it. For instance, a Neptune transit can cause lack of focus, a search for divine inspiration, and/or obsessive longings and fascinations for others. Often there is a thirst for music, inebriation and escapism in a person who could have been alienated to this mind-set previously. You might join a commune, become a better musician or artist, become a martyr or even a victim, or maybe begin a yoga practice.

During a Pluto transit over Venus a person could develop an intense, passionate or jealous, possessive mind-set within a relationship. You learn to trust your doubts. Over-all, Pluto will not let you carry on dragging an old cloak about on your shoulders. These transits can go on for years; chipping away at the crusty parts of an outmoded part of your character, which had become like a shell, hiding the real, new emerging part of you.

The life-changing larger Planets can be triggered by smaller transits to the same Natal Planet. This is often a way of glimpsing how the transit will be moving through your psyche. With astrology you come to understand the new parts of you that are growing. You are growing and becoming your better self all through your life. All through your life you are constantly adjusting to life, the meaning within you and the experiences around you. Astrology is an excellent map for this journey.

Knowing What to Look For

When the time of the transit comes you need to know what to look for. Knowing what to look for will help you to attune to the energies of the Planetary influences. When I spent years inadvertently proving the accuracy of astrology, there were times when I would deliberately not know which transits were happening. Then, looking back over my journal, I sifted the events into their synchronized causes, pinpointing the key influences.

For this journal you can get straight to the heart of the Planets' energies within you because each journal page has the key-influence written under the title of each planetary transit. Please be aware of the positive and negative manifestations of the same key-influence. How the key-influence manifests in your life is an indicator of your own inner wisdom. If the manifestation is negative, or not as positive as it could be, then this is your personal inner-growth signpost.

There is also an explanatory introduction to each transiting Planet at the beginning of each section. The astrological symbols of the transiting phenomena are also printed on the page, in a small medallion. The medallions are another way to help you learn the names and symbols of the Planets, Nodes and Angles and translate them between your horoscope and the ephemeris, to your journal.

Having preconceived ideas makes it easier to find the inner field of action which relates to a specific transit. You might think that you are tricking yourself if you are looking for it, the point is, don't trick yourself. Be open; be real, even though it may take a few months to recognize inspirations and instigations.

It is enough to be aware of unconscious processes just after they have happened. You may be aware that you are acting kind of 'funny' in the throes of unconscious behaviour. The unconscious has a particular feel to it: to me it is like a fuzzy twilight and I am centred deep inside of myself, aware of actions but not why I am doing them. Not all unconscious behaviour is bad either; there will undoubtedly be some behaviour you really are quite pleased with. The next time you do behave 'unconsciously' you won't be so unconscious. You become more and more aware of parts of you and you can then change or accept them.

It seems to me there is a never ending field of unconsciousness in every second. Like the roots of a tree. Like the currents in the oceans. The field of unconscious activity will probably be the main field of your study. You will become conscious of what was once unconscious. Where do you look? Inside your own mind, your own thoughts and feelings become clearer and clearer.

Bear in mind that transits over natal Planets are different when they are the opposite way round. For instance, a transit of Moon over Sun is different to Sun over Moon. Generally, the first will reveal a habit or need which requires integrating into consciousness; accepting and living with a part of you that had previously been unacknowledged. The latter will bring awareness of a need or habit. Similarly, Saturn transiting Mars is different to Mars transiting Saturn. In the first scenario Saturn will limit or hone successful action and in the second scenario Mars will invigorate you to take charge and do something.

Now you know when, where and what to look for, you will sail wide awake through your inner world. Your inner world is there whether you are aware of it or not. Isn't it better to be aware? Do not get caught up in judging yourself – just change what you need to. Remember you are a scientist, watching and recording impressions. This is magnificent work.

Knowing What to Write

When you know the time and you know the transit, turn to the correct page in the journal. Each page has key words and ideas for you to know what to look out for. If something happens that seems very different from the keywords then write that too. Further down the line you may learn more associations. With hindsight, you can understand an event within a realm of ideas that you were previously unaware of.

Write about your feelings, your thoughts, inspirations, realizations, ideas. Write about people, or animals, you communicate with or meet or people you try to connect with. Write about your successes and failures for that day. Write about what you enjoyed or didn't enjoy. Only you know what is going on deep in the furnaces of your soul. Write for your ears.

Whilst it is important to notice manifestations of the keywords, it is also important not to ignore what else is happening. This journal is a true study; you will not need to pretend or exaggerate or fit anything in.

After a few months you will have a lot of recordings for Moon transits and some inner Planets.

Cosmic Journal has a Facebook page or visit www.fishtailastrology.com/cosmic-journal to share your findings and read about what other people are discovering.

MOON Transits

☽

MOON TRANSITS

The Moon transits the whole horoscope once a lunar month so perhaps the feelings you will come across will be easily recognized, as they will have happened many times.

The Moon brings a feeling like a need or an emotion. It is not necessarily loud but it can spur you to a small action which may seem like nothing much; such as ringing your mother, choosing to work or staying in or greeting people like you are on top of the world. You will notice that nearly always the same transit inspires the same thing.

Our emotional nature is entwined with our well-being and so little things like tidying our house or doing a weekly shop can make us feel stable, comforted and well. We start noticing life-style patterns. These are small patterns, the parts of life that are often taken for granted. If we always shop on Wednesdays but one Wednesday the Moon conjuncts Uranus, we might want to do something more exciting. Or if it conjuncts Mars, we might have a spat with another customer. But if it conjuncts Jupiter there might be nothing else we want to do except a big shop for food.

The above examples are grossly over-simplified; because if our Natal Moon is conjunct Uranus and square Mercury, we probably don't do food shopping regularly and, instead, prefer to eat take-away and quickly prepared food. The natal placement of our Moon, with its aspects, constellation and House will provide the field of action, and only over time will you learn which area is the main domain of your Moon. But within that field are the inner workings of Moon nature.

Generally though, the Moon rules inspirations, decisions and choices around food, home, comfort, family, body and habits, and affects our mood and health. Take notice of what you need.

Transiting Moon - Natal Sun

OK to be me

The way I often am

Comfortable expressing how I am

XXXV

XXXVI

Transiting Moon - Natal Moon

Cycles. Cycles of people, of feelings

Keep coming back here

The comfort I need

XXXVIII

XXXIX

Transiting Moon - Natal Mercury

Siblings, cousins, close friends

Familial communication

Need to talk deeply, personally

XLI

XLII

Transiting Moon - Natal Venus

I would like more meaning

Can I love more?

Can things be more beautiful?

Lonely/solitude or socializing?

XLIV

XLV

Transiting Moon - Natal Mars

Spice things up a bit

Is that enough?

My sexy, powerful body

What do I need to do?

XLVII

XLVIII

Transiting Moon - Natal Jupiter

Generous helpings

For me and everyone

Fitting it all in

L

LI

Transiting Moon - Natal Saturn

I would rather be alone right now

Working

Fixing and maintaining

Staying small

LIII

LIV

Transiting Moon - Natal Uranus

Of course I could create chaos

And if I must, I could stick to routine

I could add something new

But I cannot just sit here

LVI

Transiting Moon - Natal Neptune

Captured by music

Routines sway

Sea of emotions

Gentleness, a gift

LIX

Transiting Moon - Natal Pluto

I feel what I need with a determination

I will hold on to this determination

Don't mess with me

I exist and I need

LXII

LXIII

Transiting Moon - Natal North Node

Tricky this

Not sure I am quite right

But it feels sort of special

Could be important

LXVI

Transiting Moon - Natal South Node

Ahh yes I am rather comfortable

Used to this

Quite talented really

LXVIII

LXIX

Transiting Moon - Ascendant

I feel people can see me

What shall I let them see?

Familiar environment

LXXI

Transiting Moon - Descendant

My chosen few

I grace you with my favouritism

And lavish the attention I need from you...

...back

LXXV

Transiting Moon - M.C

They see I am right

Deserving

In tune with what is required

LXXVII

Transiting Moon - I.C

Stay home

Cook, tidy, prepare

Keep me and others in my nest

LXXX

SUN
transits

☉

LXXXII

SUN TRANSITS

The Sun transits and prods our integrity by highlighting parts of our life. We experience the full benefit of joy from the Sun when we find a way to integrate our spontaneous nature with the moment. The moment can bring anything; the moment cannot be prepared for except through confidence and self-belief. The Sun represents confidence, self-belief, spontaneity and integrity. When the time comes we will stand up, be ourselves, and respond fully.

The inner strength and childishness of the Sun nature is ever-flowering as new character expressions and new ways of being are integrated. Everything offers the Sun opportunity to grow. Age, death, a walk in the park, huge projects – everything. The Sun is like the eternal child forever discovering a new way of being, expressing untried and untested behaviours in response to the ever-changing moment.

But if our Sun is afflicted with a sense of lacking or tremulousness it might be difficult to experience the joy. At least through watching transits you can see what you are pushing away, then over time, bring in self-belief and trust.

Sun signs have a lot of power and influence in our lives as it is the part of us which is inspiring, individual and a guiding light. But if people follow us they lose themselves, just as we lose ourselves if we blindly copy others. Individually we have to find trust in ourselves. Individually we grow the way we grow in response to our own ever changing moment.

Take notice of being present.

Transiting Sun – Natal Sun

Happy Birthday!

Spontaneity – check

Because you deserve it

Transiting Sun - Natal Moon

Wake-up!

This is a brand new day

Let's do it again

The way I like things

Transiting Sun - Natal Mercury

Speak truth

Blind them with words

Is this journey worth it?

Transiting Sun - Natal Venus

Mirror mirror

I see your flaws

Your beauty too

Value and play

Transiting Sun - Natal Mars

Let's do it!

Whoa! So right!

Yes! Dare

Transiting Sun - Natal Jupiter

Encouraging, there is abundance

I am in it

Lush, lucky

Transiting Sun - Natal Saturn

Great wise being

Room for manoeuvre within traditions

Lighten up a bit

Transiting Sun - Natal Uranus

Hello friend, alien, animal

What is new?

Fantastic idea

Wired today

Transiting Sun - Natal Neptune

Religion of our fathers

Kind men

Space to experience divine

Flowing

Escape

Transiting Sun - Natal Pluto

Things need changing

Renovating

Conforming to my will

Transiting Sun - Natal North Node

Other people can and do

Make space for future

Here

Now

Transiting Sun - Natal South Node

Must've been reincarnated

I am that good here

Even if it's bad

I effectively do it

Transiting Sun - Ascendant

Shine on me moving

In action, animating

This body, this way

Transiting Sun - Descendant

So glad you are here

You are vibrant

Good to be with

Transiting Sun - M.C

The way to heaven is through me

I am pointing up

A conduit for ambition

XCVIII

Transiting Sun - I.C

Home is where my heart is

The threshold shines

Retreat

Hold court

MERCURY transits

☿

MERCURY TRANSITS

When Mercury transits, in the horoscope, inner energy is triggered to communicate. Mercury moves through words, via wind, or bodily transported via car or tube or bus or web.

The principle of Mercury is to transport concepts and ideas. Whether that idea is in a person or in their mind, Mercury moves itself nearer its reception. Communication through a slight warm touch of a hand, a wicked stare, an out flow of words, and an advertising pitch are all moving flashes of thought.

What is the message? Mercury's realm is the message. The meaning in the symbol; the thoughts conveyed by warm hands or glaring eyes, the presence of a body strong and supportive are some of the myriad of ways a message can be given.

Transits by Mercury are opportunities to give or receive or share meanings. They can be apparently trite, such as 'eating aubergines is a good thing', only to later discover it opened the conversation with someone else.

How you communicate is shown by the House, constellation and aspects of Natal Mercury. Transiting Mercury comes unencumbered by any of your learned inhibitions or ways but you might find yourself choosing to use the same track of mind you have already learned. Also, the Planets' House, constellation and aspect that is being transited by Mercury, may be open or closed to the Messenger. Take notice of what you are thinking.

Transiting Mercury - Natal Sun

Messages

Reveal what is hidden

Shine on a bigger picture

Transiting Mercury - Natal Moon

Needing to communicate

Feeling the sense of connection

Belonging

Reaching out

Transiting Mercury - Natal Mercury

Letters and emails

Telephone calls and conversations

Conveying thoughts and small journeys

Transiting Mercury - Natal Venus

Network, socialize

Chatting away smiling

Pleasantly expressive in company

Transiting Mercury - Natal Mars

Either someone narks you with their words

Or you nark them

And so on

Or, you start

So you say what you want carefully

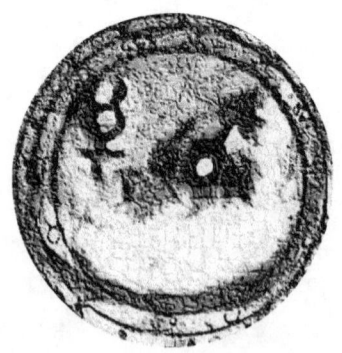

Transiting Mercury - Natal Jupiter

Flexible thinking

Big ideas, meaningful connections

Travelling

Earth, land, roads

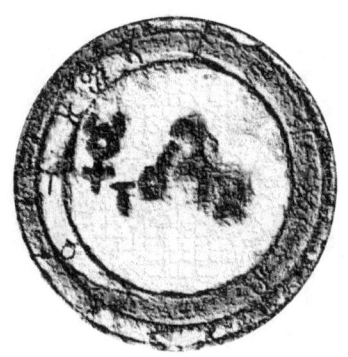

Transiting Mercury - Natal Saturn

Focus

Check accounts, paperwork

Authority, old people

Small print

Transiting Mercury - Natal Uranus

Possibly very exciting

Probably probable

Interest, invent

In...

Transiting Mercury - Natal Neptune

Listening to music

Words that sway

Sounds which awaken fascination

Stories and dreams

Transiting Mercury - Natal Pluto

Words to make change

Insight

Psychological

Hidden truths

Transiting Mercury - Natal North Node

Read new articles

Honour future maybe's

Adverts for new skills

Transiting Mercury - Natal South Node

Always talking this way

Thinking this way

Good at it

Wanting more; but what?

Transiting Mercury - Ascendant

I am saying what I am about

Where I am going

Today, tomorrow, next year

What image do I give?

Transiting Mercury - Descendant

Get a word in edgeways

Straight to their ears

Make that call, send that message

Transiting Mercury - M.C

How did you hear about me?

Yes I can do that

This is how it can be done

Let all the relevant people know

Transiting Mercury - I.C

House meeting

Message to do something different

Familial ways of interaction

Family visiting

Thoughts over the threshold

VENUS transits

♀

CXVIII

VENUS TRANSITS

Just about all of the Venus transits are enjoyable. If they are not, it is because you are blocking pleasurable feelings coming into your life.

Venus transits specifically bring a pleasant sense of well-being and value to your integrated sense of self. This is because feeling good about ourselves is an integral part of being human. We are driven to find happiness. We are driven to treasure values. Yet Venus does not drive. Venus attracts. So the realm of Venus is about attraction and giving. Magnetism. The currency in the realm of Venus is value. What do you value? Then that is what you attract.

Overall, the transits of Venus instil a sense of well-being, okayness, because our world feels good. We all have different values. These values are generally love, money and beauty. But also, a love of knowledge, of passion, of trains or rabbits. What we value attracts more of what we value.

In terms of money, not everyone really values money; they value holidays, or shoes or dining out. Maybe football, or reading. Perhaps deep conversations. So what fills that person's life? Exactly.

So don't force yourself to focus on love, money or beauty only. They are atypical values. Venus transits help you to uncover the things that really are valuable for you.

Venus awakens you to the value in each Planet it transits. Take notice of what you enjoy. Also enjoy being as attractive as you can be; it is a very natural part of us to be our most attractive; fluff your feathers!

Transiting Venus - Natal Sun

Typically Sun sign

A sure sign that the Sun sign is important

Dare to trust

Bright attraction

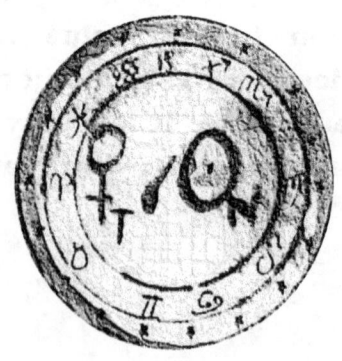

Transiting Venus - Natal Moon

One of the finest transits

Feeling lovely

Lush

Gorgeous

Comfortable

A definite love vibration

Transiting Venus - Natal Mercury

Charm; or at least the will to be pleasant

Smooth over cracks, by accepting them

Music and art with a message

Transiting Venus - Natal Venus

The day to gage the state of your love realm

Giving and receiving

Balanced? Unsatisfying? Obvious really

Transiting Venus - Natal Mars

Adorn, desire to compete

Sexual guiles

Creativity

Nice way of doing it

Transiting Venus - Natal Jupiter

Too lush to do much

Pleasure round every corner

Extravagance and ease

Philosophically giving in to desire

A pleasant journey

Transiting Venus - Natal Saturn

Beautifing the ritual

Long lasting relationships

Financial investments

Aging gracefully

Transiting Venus - Natal Uranus

Unique beauty, that little touch

Loving pets

Good friends and outrageous style

Transiting Venus - Natal Neptune

Meditation and transcendental experience

Never getting there

A beauty so profound it aches

Danger of collapsing in escape

Transiting Venus - Natal Pluto

Power and love, more powerful with love

Transforming power of everything sweet

Manipulative

Cunning sense of well being

Transmute cunning to compassion, if you can

Transiting Venus - Natal North Node

Ease into a new experience

Make the awkwardness beautiful

Ambience

Transiting Venus - Natal South Node

Natural beauty

A relief to let the guard down

Reap the same patch

Easy behaviour

Transiting Venus - Natal Ascendant

A new style

More expressive of self

A must have – like it belongs with me

Creating or finding those little flairs

Transiting Venus - Natal Descendant

In an ideal world your lover walks in and gives affection

Chances are you give it

Caring for important others

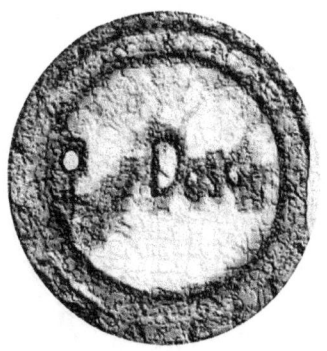

Transiting Venus - Natal M.C

A good day to get married

My corner of the world values what I value

Artists' exhibition preview

Beautifying something at work

Transiting Venus - Natal I.C

Grace all those who cross my threshold

With fair attention

Value what is little

Order, nest

Begin a new cycle to being a more loving being

MARS transits

♂

MARS TRANSITS

When Mars transits, expect to be moved, motivated and inspired to take action. Holding back at this time brings depression in its wake. Though obviously, the kind of action you take should be considered. Mars is not necessarily a spontaneous lash out in anger. Mars definitely rules anger; but how you deal with the energy of the anger is your responsibility.

Anger is a sign that your boundary has been overstepped. Instead of war, just strengthen your boundary! Fighting is not justified. Finding a way to keep what is yours and maintaining your boundary is important work. Anger belongs to Mars but Mars is the henchman of the Sun. Your Sun rules. Your Sun shines with true confidence. How you integrate anger and still get your way is your work. Mars has many tactics, dependant on constellation.

The speciality of Mars is a meaningful goal. Mars gives us our mojo and motivation through wanting to do something. You only want to do what matters to you. If your will is repeatedly knocked you will have a showdown with your soul as your personality crumbles; do you really want that? It may be that your will had saturated other people's desires and a transit shows you that you are a bit of a bully. Mars is passion and energy. Do not be lazy in acting for your true desires. The despair, depression and disappointment of an unlived Mars is far, far worse than the fall from failure.

As Mars transits your horoscope you get to look at what matters to you and how you are going about getting it. You get an influx of energy to do something more.

Often Mars brings anger, but it also brings the passion and desire to complete something for yourself. Take notice of what you want.

Transiting Mars - Natal Sun

Not much can stop you today

Motivated

Self-belief strengthened

Effort energized

Transiting Mars - Natal Moon

Passionate desires

Sexy oomph

Rashes and fevers

Physical needs

Transiting Mars - Natal Mercury

Argumentative, debating

Just saying, must say

Rushing journey

Speed, brilliance and danger

Transiting Mars - Natal Venus

Acting upon attraction

Effort to make money

Creative pursuits

Defending, upholding values

Transiting Mars - Natal Mars

This day or two is the seed day for the beginning of a new project, or new turn in existing project. It is the main precursor of depression if you do not take steps to uphold your magnificent life potential and take necessary action to do what you want without harming anyone.

Transiting Mars - Natal Jupiter

Strength and prowess

Energy to execute big ideas

Motivated to explore, journey, travel

Seek philosophical answers

Transiting Mars - Natal Saturn

Kick start, keep going

Add a switch, metal-work

Motivate old bones

Try to push beyond limitations, carefully

Triumph

Transiting Mars - Natal Uranus

Dare to pursue your idea

Quick off the start

Defending individuality

Flourish

CXLV

Transiting Mars - Natal Neptune

Motivated to meditate

Dance like a dervish

Desire to appease, do a good turn

Transiting Mars - Natal Pluto

Bold move to prove

Reaction to or against power

Trip wire trigger for boundaries

Rage

Transiting Mars - Natal Ascendant

Red in the face; anger, embarrassment

Be true to who you are

Winner, fighter, energy

Transiting Mars - Natal Descendant

Arguments

Sexy, fiery other

Overstepped boundaries

Defending boundary

Transiting Mars - Natal North Node

The sign and house of North Node is strengthened

Respond anew

Uphold behaviours which have good consequences

Defend your right to try, despite lack of support

Transiting Mars - Natal South Node

Typical anger

Stroppy, salty, terse

Determined to do what you want

Taking without asking

Transiting Mars - M.C

Jumping up to be counted

Job interviews and career moves

Sport, challenges, games, fights

Righteousness

Transiting Mars - I.C

Ending something to begin something

Practice small, at home, unseen

Arguments and tussles behind doors

Accentuating thresholds

JUPITER transits ♃

JUPITER TRANSITS

Jupiter transits, as well as Venus transits, mark some of the loveliest and most pleasant days.

Jupiter brings hope, enthusiasm and joy. Jupiter also governs the realm of the higher mind and bestows a hunger for experience and a thirst for knowledge. Jupiter brings an optimistic world-view governed by reason.

The sense of freedom associated with Jupiter comes from a reasonable insight of accepting or fleeing limitations. The associations of travel come from exploring the world around, wanting to experience, associate and interact with more of the world.

Jupiter bigs things up. The only negative association of Jupiter is with cancer; it seems to correlate with tumours growing. Also, not making a commitment because of not wanting to lose freedom could be another negative; as could the braggadocio characteristic. However, the sense of being emotionally buoyant is often impeded through up-bringing, and so it is more likely you will not allow yourself to go too far or act out the more negative expressions of Jupiter. Being interested in life is a state of mind that is, as astrology shows, a natural state of mind. Jupiter is a wonderful teacher, who praises and encourages us to be our best.

When a transit of Jupiter occurs, it is an opportunity to experience this lighter state of mind. Transits of Jupiter are also known to be lucky.

Take notice of your good-nature.

Transiting Jupiter - Natal Sun

The year this transit occurs sends ripples of excitement through our being, as the waves of Jupiter's optimism realign our mind and spirit.

And life is very good.

Transiting Jupiter - Natal Moon

Ohh the eating which occurs at this time!

Gorgeous friends, opportunities

Comfort, everything we need

Transiting Jupiter - Natal Mercury

Writing is starred

So much to say

Travel, exploration

Listening, languages

Transiting Jupiter - Natal Venus

Abundance of love, money, pleasure

Beautiful surroundings

Relaxed and lucky

Transiting Jupiter - Natal Mars

Good muscle tone

Hand-eye co-ordination

Loads of energy

Transiting Jupiter - Natal Jupiter

Every 12 years your lucky year (Chinese)

Everything you do is tinged with enthusiasm

More effort

Self-belief

Transiting Jupiter - Natal Saturn

Expertise and wisdom

Energy and authority

Successful enterprise

Idea to fruition

Transiting Jupiter - Natal Uranus

Encouraging originality

Standing up for ideas

Brilliant, innovative

Breaking old patterns

Freedom

Transiting Jupiter - Natal Neptune

Exquisite sense of joy

Inspired to mystical meanings

Deep mind

Abundance of water and music

Transiting Jupiter - Natal Pluto

Inner healing

Faith, recovery

Positive change

Energy to do what needs to be done

Transiting Jupiter - Natal North Node

The future is now

New experiences for a skillset

Inner truth

Transiting Jupiter - Natal South Node

Freedom from old patterns

Repeating old patterns excessively

Letting go with ease

Transiting Jupiter - Ascendant

Name change

Better identity

Coming out, starting over

Happy to be me

Eating too much

Transiting Jupiter - Descendant

Lucky to meet beneficial other

Generous, open, honest

Successful law case

Freedom from limitations imposed by others

Transiting Jupiter - M.C

A plan for success

Energy for work

Theatrical turns in front of a generous audience

CLXX

Transiting Jupiter - I.C

More space at home

Room for new beginnings to be practiced

Visitors

Freedom from limitations within the family

SATURN transits ♄

SATURN TRANSITS

Where Mars urges us to action and Jupiter expands our field of opportunity, Saturn enforces limitation. Suddenly, what was once joyful becomes hard work, and it may even seem to be necessary to leave it.

Saturn sharpens our mind to a critical view, honing in on detail, noticing the rubbish others would pass as OK. Saturn is a hard task-master and a life-changer.

Sometimes Saturn brings a gloom, through thoughts or loneliness. The grief Saturn can bring is saying goodbye to something old – usually an out-grown part of us that is no longer practical. Or it could be an old part of our system that is an extravagant waste of energy, considering that more important matters now need attending to.

Yet Saturn is a best friend to those who listen; Saturn brings discipline, perseverance, realistic expectations, time management, up-holding of tradition and wise authority.

Also, the fear that is often experienced with Saturn could well turn out to be a message not to go a certain way, because other things are more important and need that energy.

Saturn speaks to us through fear, loneliness and negative thoughts. Saturn does not even complement its own great wisdom; instead, it acknowledges its own authority stoically.

These transits urge us to develop a greater responsibility towards our own life. If there is a loss of energy at this time, it could be a disease; but probably it is an unconscious ploy to stop wasting time by messing around and choose a course of action and stick with it.

Notice the acceptance of life's harsh realities.

Transiting Saturn - Natal Sun

Lifting a veil in the Natal Sun's house

Laying bare realities

Focus on maintenance

The errors of your Sun sign

Getting real, staying in the moment

Transiting Saturn - Natal Moon

Impending sense of separation

Insecurity, needs not being met

Coolness

Mother yourself, kindly

Transiting Saturn - Natal Mercury

Depressing thoughts

Obsessive minutiae

Exacting speech, focused attention

Essays and other writing projects

Transiting Saturn - Natal Venus

Exposure of falsity, loneliness

Financial tightness

Be your own best friend,

Save for a rainy day, frugality, waste not

Long lasting love

Transiting Saturn - Natal Mars

Recognition of difficulty

Effort, frustration, determination

Boundaries, marking territory

Going too slow or steady?

Transiting Saturn - Natal Jupiter

Manifest big ideas

Limit excessiveness

Stick to the trodden path

Measured expansion

Transiting Saturn - Natal Saturn

Checking position

Accepting age and limitations

Re-calculating steady course

CLXXX

Transiting Saturn - Natal Uranus

Materializing genius invention

Owning individuality

Responsible and original

Limiting stupid ideas

CLXXXI

Transiting Saturn - Natal Neptune

Manifesting divine, ideal art or music

Meditation practice

Swimming lessons

Kicking the habit

Letting go of the lie

Transiting Saturn - Natal Pluto

Determined change

Unnecessary force, inner transformation

Ending of things long gone

Transiting Saturn - Natal North Node

Probably a failed attempt to bring future practice into flow

Failure part of the process

Getting it right

Trying an inspired new way

Transiting Saturn - South Node

Unacknowledged limitation

Treading same wheel

A lot of effort for natural skill

Cutting the dross away

Transiting Saturn - Ascendant

Grown-up, taking responsibility

Going it alone

Busy managing transformation

Braving the light

Transiting Saturn - Descendant

Cutting away bad habits with important people

Being real with others

Recognizing other people's limitations

Painful loss

Transiting Saturn - M.C

Deserved success or failure

Obvious efforts exposed

Craving acknowledgement

Accepted authority and experience

Transiting Saturn - I.C

Chooses limitation, acceptance of loss

Be small

Stay home

Maintain core

URANUS

transits

♅

URANUS TRANSITS

The transits of Uranus are said to be suddenly effective when it is within a degree of the astrological body being transited. Astrologers attribute the sudden impact of Uranus to prolonged disgruntlement that has been accepted as the norm: then, when Uranus reaches its specific degree, the native acts decisively without consultations. Uranus rules the realm of originality and independence, which has the state of mind of deferring to their own judgement; no-one else needs to be consulted.

Uranus transits also bring excited, wired feelings which often wake you in the night with profound ideas. It is a good idea to keep a notebook by the bed during these transits.

You may not feel particularly daring or a creative force but other people will instinctively recognize your power to behave erratically and possibly disruptively. Even if you are projecting this nature on to someone else you are probably acting disruptively, causing people to be wary of you.

Unexpected things occur under the dominion of Uranus. In fact, your need for excitement might be so strong you seek the unusual and thrilling experiences.

Uranus represents speed and flying, also creative thinking. There is a desire to be more awake, whilst taking part in new experiences.

Brilliant ideas, technology, pets (and even aliens) bring new experiences. Fighting for the under-dog, campaigning against the status-quo and being reckless are ways of expressing daring and a treasured sense of uniqueness.

Transiting Uranus - Natal Sun

Me. Myself. I

Unusual, daring and spontaneous

Yes!

Strange hair colours

Transiting Uranus - Natal Moon

Comfortably out of comfort zone

Freedom from home

Exciting new environment

Disruption to needs

Breaking out of the pattern

Transiting Uranus - Natal Mercury

Bursting with excitement

Interest in all things

Maths, physics, genius, friends, ideas

New ideas, innovations, original thinker

Transiting Uranus - Natal Venus

Independent women become prominent

Autonomous and daring displays of affection

Unusual hobbies and creativity in time with the spirit of the age

Uncommitted, flirtatious, changes in values

Transiting Uranus - Natal Mars

Displays of masculinity with daring

On/off bursts of energy and interest

Urge for excitement

Untamed animal

Unrulable

Transiting Uranus - Natal Jupiter

Insatiable appetite for something different

Traversing further afield

Search, seeking meaning

Trump analysis of philosophy and religion with autonomy

Transiting Uranus - Natal Saturn

Shaking up tradition

Renovating the old unsympathetically

Long term project taking off, or collapsing

Broken bones

Improve efficiency

Transiting Uranus - Natal Uranus

84 years old! (One full cycle of Uranus)

Or mid-life crisis (opposition)

No-one bites you

It's your life

Transiting Uranus - Natal Neptune

A generational movement

Untangling the wooliness

Shaking out the pretence

Transiting Uranus - Natal Pluto

A generational movement

Energy to discard the unnecessary

The wild animal's proof of power

Brilliant transformation

Science enabling changes

CCI

Transiting Uranus - Natal North Node

Amazing possibilities

Technological skills

Forward thinking

Spirit of the Age

Transiting Uranus - Natal South Node

Photographs and other digitalized media for posterity

Break from the past

Disruption

Danger of throwing the baby out with the bath water

Transiting Uranus - Ascendant

Piercings, coloured hair, tie-dyed clothes

Festivals and travellers

New-new!-age

Even new-age is old hat

Exciting presentation

Transiting Uranus - Descendant

Other people can be so disruptive

Or exciting

Meeting inspiring people

Challenged to accept other's individuality

Transiting Uranus - M.C

Fit in if you never fit in

Drop out if you were always in

Change of status

Transiting Uranus - I.C

House needs repair

Disruption in the home

Pets

Exciting home life

Move abroad or far away or a very different home life

NEPTUNE transits

♆

NEPTUNE TRANSITS

Neptune transits are so sweet, if you like that insatiable desire for something intangibly divine that can barely be expressed. You end up captivated, day-dreaming, touching the curled edges of a retreating vision. Whether you do or you don't, it makes sense to allow for day-dreaming time.

Listening to music, meditation, inspired dancing and the arts will be a source of relaxation from the desire to find the unfindable.

During this time the world can be perceived as devoid of real beauty and some try to escape. They drink, take drugs, gamble, and tell lies and cheat. Others make the best art they ever made. Religions are sought and sanctuaries are discovered. Shrines are erected. This is a time to make time for the divine.

During Neptune transits the world seems harsh. Water eases the roughness. Swimming and beaches call, with the waves swooshing back and forth, frothing, in constant flux, like your mind.

Stories are invented and poetry sought to ease the soul, by poets who lived tossed by the fascinations, obsessions and desires for the untouchable. Neptune transits connect you, once again, to the sense of oneness in life and to the feeling that there is more to life than just this material world.

Gratitude and compassion can over-flow and bring tears to your eyes. Sometimes, if your eyes are bleary, someone might take advantage of you.

Transiting Neptune - Natal Sun

A mesmerising sense of becoming

Filled with gratitude

Reaching out to help others

Changing jobs, tack or recognizing something creative or divine needs a permanent place in your life

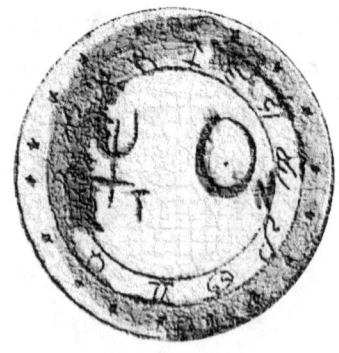

Transiting Neptune - Natal Moon

Need for fluidity

Flowing with family

Divine mothers, men in touch with feelings

Aching for a belonging with true kin

Transiting Neptune - Natal Mercury

Stories and poetry, creative writing

Awareness of speaking inner truth

Mystical texts

Amazing conversations

Elusive, vague and confusing thoughts, speech and situations

Transiting Neptune - Natal Venus

Heightened sense of beauty

Moved within by an aching desire

Longing, limerence, infatuation, fascination

Elusive love, oneness

Day-dreaming and creative imaginings

Transiting Neptune - Natal Mars

Fuzzy boundaries

Sacrificial pursuits

Magnetic and charismatic

Search for divine, some seek alcohol

Swimming/ yoga

Transiting Neptune - Natal Jupiter

Transcendental joy

Kinder world view

Mystical side of religious practices

Relaxed, positive, life affirming

Transiting Neptune - Natal Saturn

Lightening the load, easing ambition

Pleasurable chores and work

Freedom within limitations

A vision sent for manifestation

Transiting Neptune - Natal Uranus

A generational movement

Rounding the edges

Compassion within individuality

Helping less adapted individuals become more autonomous

Transiting Neptune - Natal Neptune

Water, swimming, prayers

Candles, Mystics

Transcendent

Other world

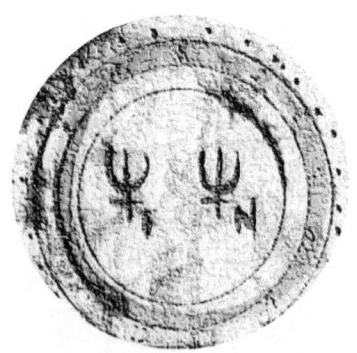

Transiting Neptune - Natal Pluto

A generational movement

Transformation through spiritual practices

Vagueness and confusion around power

Transiting Neptune – Natal North Node

Fascination to reach somewhere

Imagining being better

Searching

Transiting Neptune – Natal South Node

Lost in reincarnations

Vague memories

Nostalgia

Confusion, delusion or modesty over talent

Volunteering and other charitable acts

Transiting Neptune - Ascendant

Being somebody more smooth, mystical, flowing and compassionate

Nautical pursuits, sea, swimming

Artist, poet, story-teller

Counsellor

Transiting Neptune - Descendant

Elusive partner, maybe they drink too much, aren't truthful

Perfect partner, idealized, romantic and fascinating

Woolly boundaries with others

Taken advantage of or equally helped beyond measure

Person with strong Neptune qualities comes into your life

Transiting Neptune – M.C

Recognized as creative, mystical

Work within the Arts or counselling

Ordained

Success with water

Vague values upheld

Retirement

Transiting Neptune I.C

Floods or leaks in the house

Extended family from over-seas

Unsure of lineage

Meditation or holistic practices in the home

Beautiful, calm home environment

Music too

PLUTO transits

PLUTO TRANSITS

This tiny Planet brings enormous consequences as it transits, back and forth, over a specific degree for years. The intensity and constancy of the universe making a point is unmistakeable. Changes and transformations occur, hopefully through choice. Pluto has a way of wresting old cloaks we treasure from our clinging grasp.

Although all transits bring transformation, the specific realm of Pluto is the id level of our psyche. This is the childish, passionate, unruly and desirous nature which tantrums when it cannot have what it wants. Pluto teaches resilience and foresight. Therefore, the power associated with Pluto is fierce.

Although Pluto represents inner power, there will be many incidences when others abuse their power over you, forcing you to respond. Hopefully, this response would be with inner-strength and not burning resentment seeking revenge, which is also linked to Pluto's realm. If you are abusing your power over others you will not experience the glorious inner strength and more profound meaning.

Pluto in the horoscope is not the underworld of the Greeks; it is deep change through readjustment to power.

Pluto does not bring change like Uranus brings a change of something different. Pluto changes things by its realignment to it. Pluto brings reformation.

The power Pluto awakens is awareness of the 'juice' within the situation or between people.

Transiting Pluto – Natal Sun

Strength, determination to be

Forcing right

Awareness of emotional currents

Transiting Pluto – Natal Moon

Using emotional awareness to effect change

Juicy exchanges

Obsessive and intense

Transiting Pluto - Natal Mercury

Hypnotism, speech altered for effect, manipulation

Throat chakra, occult texts

Intentions set at fundamental level

Clarity, piercing insight

Transiting Pluto – Natal Venus

Attractiveness used for gain

Obsessive, dark and earthy: transformational art

Jealousy and paranoia in close relationships

Damning prophesies from charlatans and other manipulations of your openness.

Transiting Pluto – Natal Mars

Determined, powerful, fear of powerlessness

Anger, force, right and might

Inner strength unsurpassed

Transiting Pluto – Natal Jupiter

Review belief system

Love and fear of God force

Fear of no God

Inner power

God, no God

Transiting Pluto – Natal Saturn

Harsh determination

Adherence to strict limitations

Difficulty letting go

Enforced changes

Transiting Pluto – Natal Uranus

A generational thing

Transformation to destroy old patterns

Including individuals

Transiting Pluto – Natal Neptune

A generational thing

Transforming the notion of spiritual tsunnamis

Engulfing emotional currents

Overcoming the gentle, the addicts or insiduous people

Transiting Pluto – Natal Pluto

Ability to accept change recognized

Watching transformations in slow motion

A generational thing

Justifies

Transiting Pluto – Natal North Node

Re-evaluation of what the future needs

Might not have enough energy to do it oneself

Others may act on your behalf

Transiting Pluto – Natal South Node

Letting go, walking on, moving away

A big pill to swallow

Facing a lifetime of corruption

Transiting Pluto – Natal Ascendant

Accepting power

Not wanting to be small and fearful anymore

Glaring eyes

Inner strength

Ability to seem invisible

Transiting Pluto – Natal Descendant

Danger of assault

Distrusting others

Owning psychological partner

Seeking deeper interactions

Transiting Pluto – Natal M.C

Social pariah or redeemed convict

Fearful, anxious career change

Magnetic authority

Transiting Pluto – Natal I.C

Upsetting changes within family

Sensitized threshold to home

Psychological renovation

Roots

NORTH NODE transits

☊

NORTH NODE TRANSITS

The North Node represents skills and talents which need to be developed for a future life. It is like an unseen support which keeps us moving through time, learning lessons and developing us into meaningful and better people.

The North Node may be difficult to follow. If, in the Natal horoscope, there is no other astrological body conjuncting the North Node, it stands alone and unsupported within a House, opposed by the karmic pull of the South Node.

Focusing on your Natal North Node is a very good practice, as it is said that developing the area of life represented by House and Sign will pull together all the other threads of your life and bind them in one skein.

The North Node has an incredibly positive, yet gentle effect. The North Node awakens the possibilities within the House of the astrological body it transits. Avenues previously not explored may be seen as simple solutions or bridges to a field of interest. This transit brings better ways of doing things as well as integrating new things which are beneficial and meaningful for the future.

Notice how your own Natal North Node brings its teachings, ideas and wisdoms through the transiting North Node.

TRANSITING SOUTH NODE: I have not included the transiting South Node because I do not watch it specifically. When I do, I have found I lose focus and interest in the realm being activated. Though I have noticed (through many charts I have watched) in times of death, shock or misfortune, the South Node has often transited previously, along with a few other transits, over a period of a few days or a week. This has led me to conclude that many, seemingly small, choices and emotional realizations are made for an incident to occur. Where South Node has a link with the concept of Karma, the South Node seems to keep us tied or helps untie knots, according to its inner rule.

Transiting North Node - Natal Sun

Add a new dimension to expressing a natural inclination

Might feel awkward; but worth the effort

Transiting North Node - Natal Moon

Grown up, calm, accepting

Nurturing with a light touch

Attendance to necessities

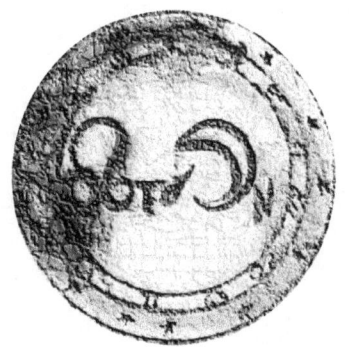

Transiting North Node - Natal Mercury

Synchronicity of advertising

Emails, words spoken, telephone calls

Apparent normality

Truths spoken, lies made clear

Transiting North Node - Natal Venus

A story unfolds

Emotional reality shared

Meeting people who are good for us

Transiting North Node - Natal Mars

Doing what you know you ought for an interesting, meaningful life

Hauling your body to begin projects

Finding your body wants to do it in another way

Transiting North Node - Natal Jupiter

Freedom to unfold

Openness to new ideas

Future benefits

CCLI

Transiting North Node - Natal Saturn

Make a commitment and save yourself

Charter a course

Take steps

Transiting North Node - Natal Uranus

Opportunity to do what excites you

But do you dare?

Is your imagination too small?

Will you take the proverbial leap?

Transiting North Node - Natal Neptune

Spiritual environment

Mystical experiences

Air of awakening

Hiding from discontent

Transiting North Node - Natal Pluto

Coolness towards power

Unaffected by mind-games

Light touch to uncover and reveal transformation

Transiting North Node - Natal North Node

How well have you developed this area of your life?

What benefits are there?

What more needs to be done?

What would you be like without these qualities?

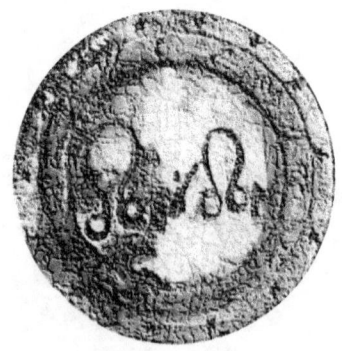

Transiting North Node - Natal South Node

Integrating new behaviours with old behaviours

Making habitual patterns more palatable

Creating space in the mind

Pauses before triggers and unthinking expressions

Transiting North Node - Ascendant

Watching how others do it and copying

Trying to act smoothly

Being smooth and careful

Seamless, natural, easy

Transiting North Node - Descendant

Other people who are good for you

Keeping in touch or saying goodbye is not the issue

Sharing what is real at that time

Transiting North Node - M.C

Seen as an individual in your own right, with all your facets and accepting all your roles, you take each part responsibly.

Transiting North Node - I.C

Returning home

Beginning a new way

Letting go of the old

Practicing in private

Using home productively

PREPARING FOR TRANSITS

The following pages are to prepare transits for the future. This practice helps prepare your mind for a way through changes ahead. For instance, if Uranus will transit your Moon and soon after Jupiter crosses your I.C and Saturn comes up to conjuncting your Mercury, you could meld their concepts together and see a process of finding a place to live that includes space for reflection and fun. If you do not consider the later transits, of Jupiter and Saturn, the Uranus transit conjunct Moon could force you to move suddenly with unnecessary upheaval and no plan. Your values change. So under Uranus transit Moon you may feel you need change and excitement but with no forethought you could find yourself mentally frustrated and unsettled later. This is just an example; there are other, similar, ways to interpret such a set of transits. The more you use your imagination the more possibilities will open up.

Astrologers use the time before a transit to till the soil and sow the seeds. Then when the time of the transit occurs, they reap the harvest. Astrologers work with clients leading them to deep, inner work. The client becomes more involved and aware of the part of their psyche they are working on. As individual astrologers you will work with a Planet of your choice, by exploring that Planet's nature within you. Imagination is the key which will open door after door. Your birth chart is the map which will save you going down one rabbit hole after another. Use your birth chart to keep returning to the umbrella meaning of the Planet.

Sometimes you will get a dream image of an archetype which expresses the astrological concept you had been working on. If you like it you can imagine living it. If you do not like it then unpick it more, from the fabric of your mind.

Astrological work is wonderful work. Your horoscope is your best counsellor. It reflects back every issue you raise and asks how you want it to be. Astrology is used to transmute our inner world to create the life attuned to us. We can trust our horoscope to not lead us astray, as we learn to trust ourselves to be the best we can be.

DATE	TRANSIT

NOTES: **notes about notes: new concepts, new ideas to check out later: draw the symbols and make them my own: the symbol which fascinates me most right now is....fascinations change as I develop: notes about other people who bring out a Planetary energy in me: notes:**

CCLXIX

Also published by Fishtail Arts & Astrology:

Manual of Astrological Calculations 2019

Astro Journal 2018

Just Cosmic 2018

Age of the Fishtail 2013

www.fishtailastrology.com

FB Fishtail Arts & Astrology

Cosmic Journal by Rikki Blythe

Published by Fishtail Arts & Astrology

 2018